Outdoor Knots

A Pocket Guide to the Most Common Knots,
Hitches, Splices, and Lashings

CLIFF JACOBSON

ILLUSTRATIONS BY LON LEVIN

FALCONGUIDES

GUILFORD. CONNECTICUT

FALCONGUIDES®

An imprint of The Rowman & Littlefield Publishing Group, Inc.
4501 Forbes Blvd., Ste. 200
Lanham, MD 20706
www.rowman.com
Falcon and FalconGuides are registered trademarks and Make Adventure
Your Story is a trademark of The Rowman & Littlefield Publishing
Group, Inc.

Distributed by NATIONAL BOOK NETWORK

British Library Cataloguing in Publication Information available

Library of Congress Cataloging-in-Publication Data

Names: Jacobson, Cliff, author. | Levin, Lon, illustrator.
Title: Outdoor knots : a pocket guide to the most common knots, hitches,
    splices, and lashings / Cliff Jacobson ; illustrations by Lon Levin.
Other titles: Basic illustrated knots for the outdoors
Description: Guilford, Conn. : FalconGuides, 2019. | Revised edition of:
    Basic illustrated knots for the outdoors. 2008
Identifiers: LCCN 2018045280 (print) | LCCN 2018047845 (ebook) |
ISBN 9781493041947 (e-book) | ISBN 9781493041930 (pbk. : alk.
paper) Subjects: LCSH: Knots and splices. | Rope. Classification: LCC
VM533 (ebook) | LCC VM533 .J34 2019 (print) | DDC
    623.88/82—dc23
LC record available at https://lccn.loc.gov/2018045280

∞™ The paper used in this publication meets the minimum require-
ments of American National Standard for Information Sciences—
Permanence of Paper for Printed Library Materials, ANSI/NISO
Z39.48-1992.

Printed in the United States of America

To Bob Roman, a gentle, courageous man

Contents

CHAPTER 1

Choosing Rope

To most people a rope is a rope, and they make no distinction between natural or synthetic fibers. That's too bad, because certain rope materials and weaves excel in certain applications. The following are some things to consider when choosing ropes.

Flexibility. Flexible ropes accept knots more willingly than stiffer weaves, but when coiled they are more likely to twist and snag. Choose flexible ropes for tying gear on cars, for general utility, and wherever a proper lashing is needed. Ropes with a stiff "hand" are best for lifeguard throwing lines and use around water.

Slipperiness. A slippery rope is always a nuisance. Polyethylene and polypropylene ropes are so slippery that they retain knots only if you lock them in place with a whipping or security hitch.

Diameter versus strength. The rule of thumb says that if you double the diameter of a rope, you quadruple its strength. This estimate can be refined with tabular data from the Cordage Institute (www.ropecord.com). For comparison: New ¼-inch three-strand nylon rope yields a tensile strength of 1,490 pounds; ½-inch nylon rope of similar construction tests at 5,750 pounds.

Safe working load. Safety factors and working loads are not the same for all types of rope or applications, so it is not possible to accurately define "safe working load." The important thing to remember is that estimated working loads like those listed in table 1 are simply *guidelines* to product selection. They naturally assume that ropes are in good condition and are being used in noncritical applications under normal service conditions. Suggested working loads should always be reduced where there is danger to life or property or when the rope will be exposed to shock or sustained stress.

Table 1: Estimated Working Loads

	Tensile Strength	Working Load
Manila	1,220	122
Sisal	1,080	108
Nylon	3,340	278
Polyester	3,340	334
Polypropylene	2,440	244
Polyester/polypropylene composite	2,430	243
Kevlar wire rope construction		3,000

Strength in pounds for some ⅜-inch diameter standard construction three-strand twisted and eight-strand plaited ropes. Working loads are for rope in good condition used in noncritical applications and under normal service conditions. These are guidelines only.

Memory. The ability of a rope to retain a coiled or knotted shape is called "memory." Lariats and throwing lines must necessarily "remember" their manners or they'll snag when played out. Generally, stiffness and good memory go hand in hand—but not always. For example, polyethylene line is very flexible, but it never forgets its store-bought windings. Most high-memory ropes don't take knots very well.

Ultraviolet degradation. This is important to consider if your ropes are exposed to sunlight for long periods of time. Table 2 on the next two pages provides the comparative specifics.

Stretch. Towing and mountaineering work demand a stretchy rope; "tie-down" applications require the opposite. Natural-fiber ropes (such as manila, hemp, and sisal) shrink when wet, while nylon ones stretch under load. Forty years ago, campers faithfully loosened natural fiber tent guylines each night before they retired. Today's campers tighten nylon ropes when the sun goes down and several times during a storm.

Floatability. Polypropylene and polyethylene (which float) are the logical choices for water-ski ropes and throwing lines.

Effects of chemicals. Spill insect repellent on polypropylene rope and you'll have a handful of mushy fiber. All ropes are affected to some degree by harsh solvents.

Table 2: Comparison of Some Common Ropes

	MANILA	SISAL	COTTON
STRENGTH:			
Breaking tenacity—dry (grams/denier)	5–6.0	4–5.0	2–3.0
Wet strength compared to dry strength	Up to 120%	Up to 120%	Up to 120%
Shock load absorption ability	Poor	Poor	Very poor
WEIGHT:			
Specific gravity	1.38	1.38	1.54
Able to float	No	No	No
ELONGATION:			
Percent at break	10–12%	10–12%	5–12%
Creep (extension under sustained load)	Very low	Very low	Very low
EFFECTS OF MOISTURE:			
Water absorption of individual fibers	Up to 100%	Up to 100%	Up to 100%
Resistance to rot, mildew, and deterioration due to marine organisms	Poor	Very poor	Very poor
DEGRADATION:			
Resistance to UV in sunlight	Good	Good	Good
Resistance to aging for properly stored rope	Good	Good	Good
ROPE ABRASION RESISTANCE:			
Surface	Good	Fair	Poor
Internal	Good	Good	Good
THERMAL PROPERTIES:			
High temperature working limit	300°F	300°F	300°F
Low temperature working limit	-100°F	-100°F	-100°F
Melts at			Chars at 300°F

[1]Grades with special overfinishes are available to enhance wet strength properties.
[2]Based on DuPont Kevlar data.
[3]Excellent when jacketed.
Specifications courtesy of the Cordage Institute (www.ropecord.com)

NYLON	POLYESTER	POLYPROPYLENE	POLYETHYLENE	ARAMISS[2]
7.8–10.4	7.0–9.5	6.5	6	18–26.5
85-90%[1]	100%+[1]	100%	105%	95%
Excellent	Very good	Very good	Fair	Poor
1.14	1.38	0.91	0.95	1.44
No	No	Yes	Yes	No
15–28%	12–15%	18–22%	20–24%	1.5–3.6%
Moderate	Low	High	High	Very low
2.0–8.0%	1.00%	None	None	3.5–7.0%
Excellent	Excellent	Excellent	Excellent	Excellent
Good	Excellent (black is best)	Fair (black is best)	Fair	Fair[3]
Excellent	Excellent	Excellent	Excellent	Excellent
Very good	Best	Good	Fair	Fair[3]
Excellent	Best	Good	Good	Good
25°F	275°F	200°F	150°F	350°F
-70°F	-70°F	-20°F	-100°F	-100°F
420–480°F	490–500°F	330°F	285°F (begins to decompose)	800°F

	MANILA	SISAL	COTTON
CHEMICAL RESISTANCE:			
Effect of acids	Will disintegrate in hot diluted and cold concentrated acids	Same as manila	Same as manila
Effect of alkalis	Poor resistance; will lose strength when exposed	Same as manila	May swell but will not be damaged
Effect of organic solvents	Fair resistance for fiber, but hydrocarbons will remove protective lubricants on rope	Good resistance	Poor resistance

Specifications courtesy of the Cordage Institute (www.ropecord.com)

NYLON	POLYESTER	POLYPROPYLENE	POLYETHYLENE	ARAMISS[2]
Decomposed by strong mineral acids; resistant to weak acids	Resistant to most mineral acids; disintegrate by 95% sulphuric acid	Very resistant	Very resistant	Resistant to most weak acids. Strong acids will attack, particularly at high temperatures or concentrations.
Little or none	No effect cold; slowly disintegrate	Very resistant	Very resistant	Resistant to most weak alkalis. Strong alkalis will attack, particularly at high temperatures or concentrations.
Resistant, soluble to some phenolic compounds and in 90% formic acid	Generally unaffected; soluble in some phenolic compounds	Soluble in chlorinated hydrocarbons at 160°F	Same as polypropylene	Resistant to most ketones, alcohols, oils, hydrocarbons

Types of Rope

Nylon. The most popular rope fiber, nylon is strong, light, immune to rot, and shock absorbent. The most popular weaves are *three strand twisted* and *braided* or *sheathed* (figure 1). Twisted rope strands unravel when heated and are therefore difficult to flame-whip when cut. They are best whipped with waxed string, plastic whipping compound, or heat-shrunk plastic tubing.

Braided (sheathed) rope is actually two ropes, one inside the other. It's wonderfully pliable, and it resists twists and kinks when coiling. Braided rope flame-whips easily, and its casing resists abrasion; however, its sheath may mask flaws in the core.

Figure 1

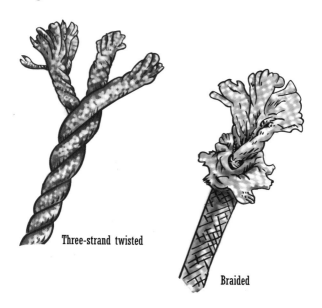

Three-strand twisted

Braided

Polyethylene. Inexpensive, slippery, slightly elastic, unaffected by water, available in colors, and it floats—popular for towing water-skiers.

Polypropylene. Similar to polyethylene but less slippery and more elastic (a better rope). Abrasion, ultraviolet light, and heat are major enemies of plastic (polypropylene and polyethylene) ropes. Not all polypropylene cordage is the same. Some types (notably baler twine) have ultraviolet inhibitors and can hold knots without slipping.

Polyester (Dacron) is the material for sailboat sheet and mooring lines and every place you need a rope that is dimensionally stable and resistant to ultraviolet light. Unlike nylon, polyester rope retains all of its strength when wet (see table 2), which is the reason sailors like it. You can get prestretched polyester rope for special applications that require extreme dismensional stability.

Natural-fiber ropes. Except for cotton, which is still used for sash cords and clothesline, natural-fiber ropes such as manila, sisal, hemp, and jute have almost gone the way of the passenger pigeon. Natural fibers have a nice hand; they coil well and hold knots tenaciously. But they rot easily and for their weight aren't very strong. For example, the tensile strength in pounds of new manila rope is roughly 8,000 times the square of its diameter in inches. Thus, new ⅜-inch manila will theoretically hold about .375 x .375 x 8,000 = 1,125 pounds (the Cordage Institute figure is 1,220)—hardly a match for the modern synthetics in table 1.

Kevlar is a gold-colored synthetic fiber developed by DuPont. It's used as a tirecord fiber, for bullet-resistant vests, and as fabrication material for ultralight canoes and kayaks. Kevlar rope is very light (its specific gravity is 1.44); it's about four times as strong as steel of the same diameter, and it is so expensive that it's recommended only for applications where extreme strength, light weight, low elongation, and noncorrosion are major concerns. Kevlar is difficult to cut, even with the sharpest tools.

Ten Most Important Knots and Hitches

1. Anchor (*fisherman's*) bend
2. Bowline
3. Butterfly noose
4. Clove hitch
5. One half hitch/two half hitches
6. Monofilament fishing knot (*clinch knot*)
7. Power cinch (*trucker's knot*)
8. Quick-release (*slippery*) loop
9. Sheet bend/double sheet bend/slippery sheet bend
10. Timber hitch

Preparing a New Rope

I wouldn't think of striking off into the backcountry without one or two 50-foot hanks of ⁵⁄₁₆-inch twisted nylon rope. On occasion, my ropes have served to extract a rock-pinned canoe from a raging rapid; to rig a nylon rain tarp in the teeth of a storm; as a strong clothesline and swimmer's rescue rope; to secure gear on my truck; and once to haul my old Volkswagen Beetle out of a knee-deep ditch.

A well-maintained rope may last a decade. An ill-kept one won't survive a season. First order of business is to seal the ends (called "whipping") by one of the following methods, so they won't unravel:

Flame-whipping. Most synthetic ropes flame-whip easily. All you need is a cigarette lighter or a small propane blowtorch. Braided (sheathed) ropes, including parachute cord, should be seared full circle, just back of the ends, then cut square through the (cooled) flamed section with a sharp blade. For a neat, trim look, finish by lightly flaming the cut end, as illustrated in figure 2. This three-step procedure will prevent the ends from cauliflowering when heat is applied.

Twisted rope tends to unravel when flame is applied. The solution is to wrap the end firmly with tape, then sear the area behind the tape all around. When the rope has cooled, remove the tape, cut the end square through the singed section, and reflame the end, as illustrated in figure 3. The length of your whipping should equal the diameter of the rope.

Figure 2

1. Flame rope half an inch back of end.

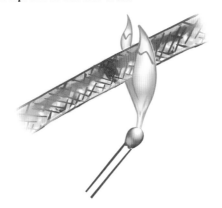

2. Cut cooled flamed section.

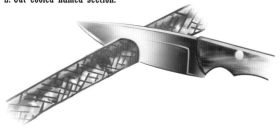

3. Reflame cut end.

Figure 3

1. Tape end.

2. Flame behind tape.

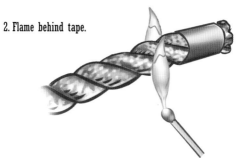

3. Cut through flamed area.

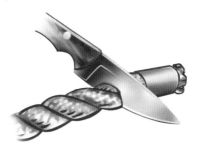

4. Reflame end.

String-whipping. Time-consuming to do but more reliable than flame or liquid plastic. The "simple whip" illustrated in figure 4 is adequate for most chores. For best results, use shoemaker's waxed thread or heavy button or carpet thread (dental floss works great) and wind against the lay of the rope, toward the end.

Figure 4

1. Make a loop lengthwise on the rope and wind evenly upward around loop and rope.

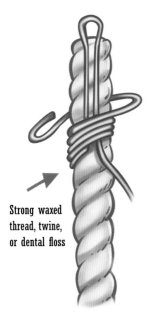

Strong waxed thread, twine, or dental floss

2. Pass free end of thread through loop.

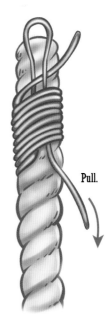

Pull.

3. Pull opposite end of thread to tighten
   loop. Cut thread flush with whipping.

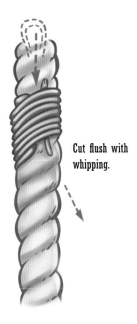

Cut flush with
whipping.

Plastic-whipping. Dip the rope end into
"liquid plastic rope whipping," and allow it to
dry. For a neater look, apply heat-shrunk plastic
sleeves to the rope ends. These products come in a
variety of colors and are available at most marinas.
For a less elegant whip, apply epoxy or electrical
tape to the end of the rope.

Coiling Your Rope for Proper Storage

On a canoe trip some years ago, one canoe swamped in a heavy rapid. There was a bouldery falls just downstream, so we had to get a throwing line to the men in the water immediately. Two 50-foot nylon ropes, which were properly coiled for throwing, were heaved to the pair who were hanging on to the gunnels of the water-filled canoe. The men caught the ropes and were rescued just 50 feet above the falls!

Figure 5. Old Navy Method

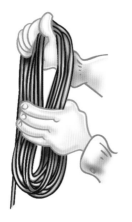

Step 1. Coil the rope: Take care to lay each coil carefully into place, twisting it a half turn so it will lay without twisting. Then, grasp the main body of the rope with one hand and place your thumb through the eye of the coils to hold them in place as shown in figure 5, step 1.

Step 2. Remove the last two coils of rope; take this long free end, and wind it around the main body of the rope several times (figure 5, step 2). Wind the free end downward, toward the hand holding the rope body. Wind evenly and snugly. Don't make the coils too tight.

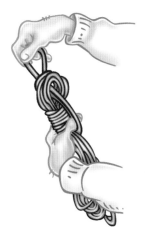

Step 3. Form a loop with the free end of the rope as shown in step 3, and push it through the eye of the rope body.

Step 4. Grasp the wound coils with one hand and the rope body with the other hand and slide the coils upward tightly against the loop. The rope is now coiled and secured (step 4). Pulling the free end of the rope will release the line, which can quickly be made ready for throwing.

Figure 6. Sailor's Stowing Coil

The sailors' stowing coil method doesn't look as neat, but it better preserves the integrity of the coils (they're less likely to snag when the rope is tossed out). **Procedure:** Coil the rope and double the last few feet to form a long loop. Wind the loop around the coil and secure with a pair of half hitches, as illustrated. Hang your rope from the loop at top.

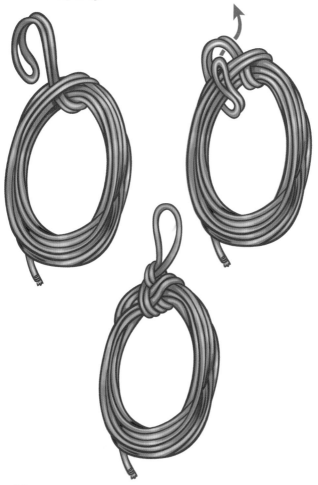

Figure 7. Rope Nomenclature

All the knots and hitches in this book may be mastered by simply following the diagrams and reading the accompanying text. You don't need to know any of these "rope terms" to understand the illustrations or descriptions. Nonetheless, no knot book would be complete without the basic nomenclature, which you may commit to memory or disregard.

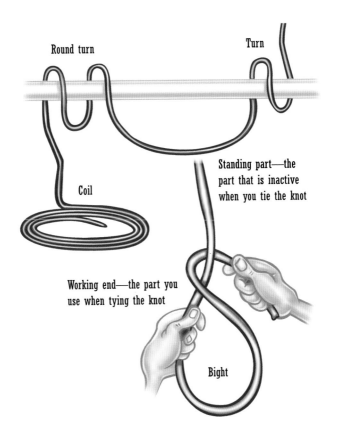

Round turn

Turn

Coil

Standing part—the part that is inactive when you tie the knot

Working end—the part you use when tying the knot

Bight

How to Care for Your New Rope

Abrasion is the kiss of death, so keep your ropes clean. I wash mine once a year in a sudsy tub of liquid detergent. Then I coil and air-dry my ropes and store them in a cool, dry place.

Tip: To remove the "memory" of store-bought coils, slightly stretch a new rope (tie it off tight between trees) for an hour or two. An old snagged rope may forget its windings if you soak it briefly in water then administer the stretch treatment.

All ropes, natural and synthetic, are injured to some extent by ultraviolet light. Keep your ropes out of the sun as much as possible.

CHAPTER 2

Knots

L eft-handed knots are indicated by the tag "Left-Handed." The left-handed knots are usually placed on the left or lower side of knot diagrams. To save space, the knots judged by the author as "universal" are illustrated in right-handed form only.

How Strong Are Knots?

All knots reduce rope strength, and some weaken it more than others. As a general rule, knots reduce rope strength by about 50 percent.

The chart on the following page indicates the approximate breaking strength, in percent, of some popular knots. A clove hitch, for example, weakens

A tight rope that winds over the sharp edge of a car bumper or piece of square steel channel or wood railing is subject to serious abrasion. An old boating trick is to insert the part of the rope that makes the bend through a length of flexible plastic tubing such as a water pipe.

the rope by about 25 percent; hence the 75 percent "breaking strength" figure for a rope with clove hitch applied.

Note that splices (which aren't really knots at all) detract barely, if at all, from a rope's breaking strength—this is why they're the preferred way to join lines.

Breaking Strength of Knots (in percent)

Anchor (*fisherman's*) bend:	70
Pipe hitch:	70
Bowline:	60
Two half hitches:	75
Bowline on a bight:	60
Sheepshank:	45
Clove hitch:	75
Square (*reef*) knot:	45
Figure eight (*end*) knot:	48
Timber hitch:	70
Monofilament fishing knot (*clinch knot*):	80
Eye splice:	95
Single overhand knot (*half a "granny"*):	45
Short splice:	90

Figures are derived from: *Plymouth Cordage*, 1946, and from tests by Scovell, Miller, Dent, Trumpler, and Day, as reported in *The Art of Knotting and Splicing*, by Cyrus Lawrence Day, 1970; and *Ropework, Practical Knots, Hitches and Splices*, by J. Grant Dent, University of Minnesota Agricultural Extension Service, USDA 1964.

Knots

Figure 8. Anchor (Fisherman's) Bend

With a breaking strength of approximately 70 percent, the anchor bend is one of the strongest knots known. It won't slip or jam, and it can be easily untied. The hitch was originally used to tie the anchor ring on sailing vessels—testimony to its reliability. Probably the best hitch to use for mooring small boats, the anchor bend also works great for securing lures to monofilament fishing line. Its one drawback is that it is difficult to make in large-diameter rope. Belt-and-suspenders folk sometimes complete the bend with a half hitch on the standing part.

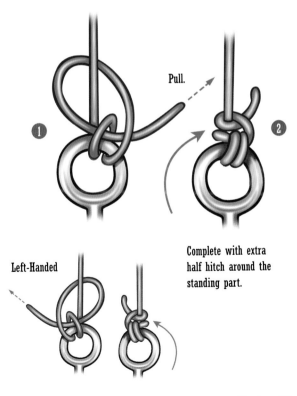

Pull.

Left-Handed

Complete with extra half hitch around the standing part.

Figure 9. Bowline

The bowline is a very secure knot that won't slip, regardless of the
load applied. It is commonly used by mountain climbers to tie their
climbing ropes around their waists. Use this knot whenever you want
to put a nonslip loop on the end of a line. Beginners are often told
to make the bowline by forming a loop, or "rabbit hole." The rabbit
(working end of the rope) comes up through the hole, around the
tree (standing part of the rope), and back down the hole. The bowline
will slip a few inches before it tightens, so allow an extra-long
working end.

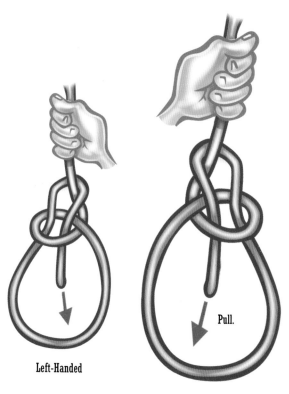

Left-Handed

Pull.

Figure 10. Locking Bowline

For complete security, especially in slippery plastic ropes, complete the bowline with two half hitches, as illustrated. This "improved bowline" is sometimes called the locking bowline. Figure 19a shows how to tie a basic half hitch.

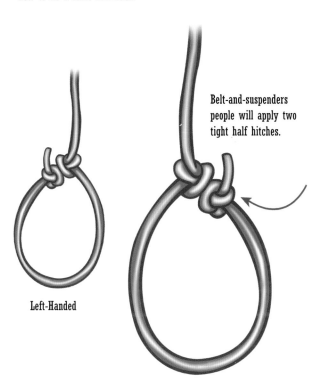

Belt-and-suspenders people will apply two tight half hitches.

Left-Handed

Figure 11. Butterfly Noose (right-handed only)

Mountain climbers use the butterfly noose to attach carabiners or whenever they need a nonslip loop in the middle of a rope. Butterfly loops are secure and will accommodate a load in any direction. They can be spaced along a line to provide purchase points for a winch line—essential in canoe rescue work. Need to pull a long rope tight? Evenly spaced butterfly nooses will give each person a secure handhold. The knot is also handy for fastening gut leaders to monofilament fishing line. Like the bowline, the butterfly noose will not jam, regardless of load direction. Also called the "lineman's loop," this knot was once popular with telephone line workers.

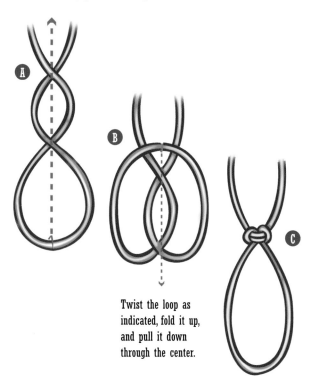

Twist the loop as indicated, fold it up, and pull it down through the center.

Figure 12. Bowline on a Bight

Use this whenever you need to make a two-legged "bosun's chair" for rescue work, or when you need a nonslip loop in the middle of a rope when both ends are inaccessible. The bowline on a bight differs from the conventional bowline in that the loop in the center of the "rabbit" (see description of bowline on page 24) is passed over the doubled loop, which is hanging below, then forced up behind the standing part of the rope. Hold the rope firmly with your left hand as you pull down with your right to tighten the knot.

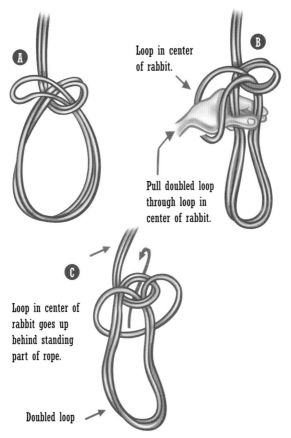

A

B

Loop in center of rabbit.

Pull doubled loop through loop in center of rabbit.

C

Loop in center of rabbit goes up behind standing part of rope.

Doubled loop

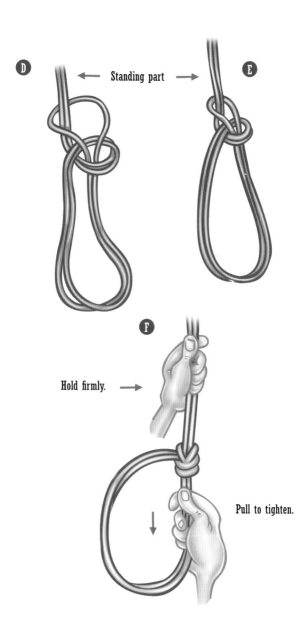

D

← Standing part →

E

F

Hold firmly. →

Pull to tighten.

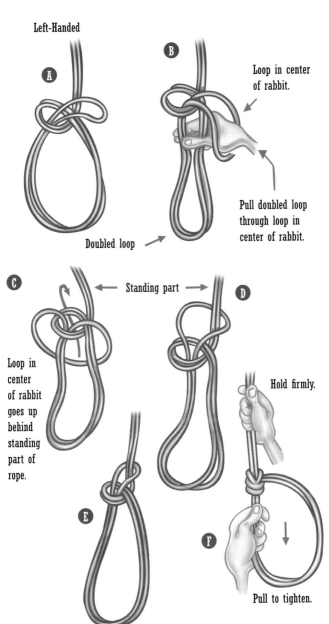

Left-Handed

A

B
Loop in center of rabbit.

Doubled loop

Pull doubled loop through loop in center of rabbit.

C
Loop in center of rabbit goes up behind standing part of rope.

Standing part

D

E

F
Hold firmly.

Pull to tighten.

Figure 13. Cat's Paw (right-handed only)

Here's a slick way to attach a rope to a hook or the towing link of a vehicle. The cat's paw is secure under heavy load, yet it comes apart easily—the reason why it remains popular with longshoremen and movers. Form two loops at the end of your rope, twist them around several times, and hook them in place. That's all there is to it.

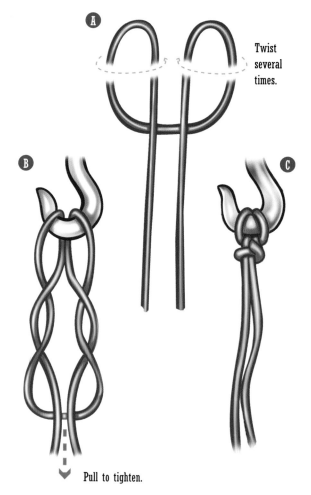

A

Twist several times.

B

C

Pull to tighten.

Figure 14. Clove Hitch

A popular knot for mooring boats to piers and pilings and securing ratlines to the shrouds on sailboats, the clove hitch is also a common "starter" knot for lashings and the diamond hitch. When absolute security is needed, finish the knot with one or two half hitches, as illustrated in Figure 14c.

 Right-Handed

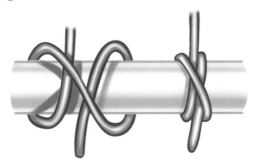

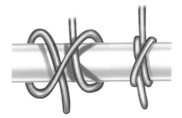 Left-Handed

To apply a clove hitch to a vertical post, use this simple method.

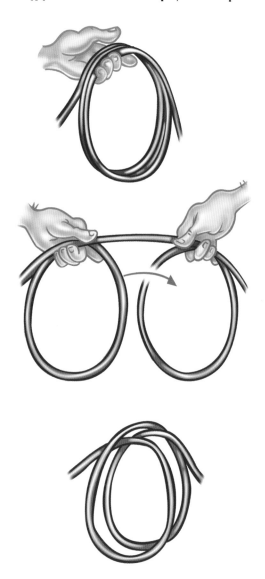

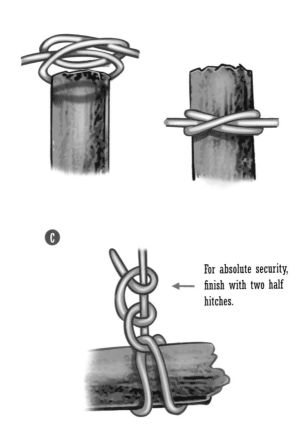

C

For absolute security, finish with two half hitches.

Figure 15. Diamond Hitch (right-handed only)

For centuries, this classic hitch has been used by prospectors, fur traders, and trappers to secure gear on pack animals. Use the diamond hitch to tie a load onto a car top or trailer: All you need is one long rope. The real value of the diamond hitch is that strain on one part of the rope is taken up elsewhere in the hitch, which causes the line to tighten. The "six-point" diamond suspension provides security even when the load shifts.

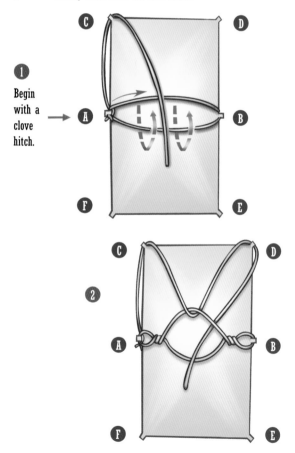

1 Begin with a clove hitch.

2

To apply a diamond hitch to a pack frame, begin by tying a rope end at point **A** using a clove hitch (see page 31). Then, loop the line around **B** and **C** as illustrated. Next, twist the horizontal center strands a couple of times and feed the working end of the rope through, looping it over the frame points in the order illustrated. When the hitch is complete, pull the rope to tighten the hitch, then tie it off where you started it with two half hitches.

Note: When tying to a pack animal, the hitch usually originates and ends at the ring in the girth strap, and the "diamond" in the center appears much larger than illustrated.

End with two half hitches. →

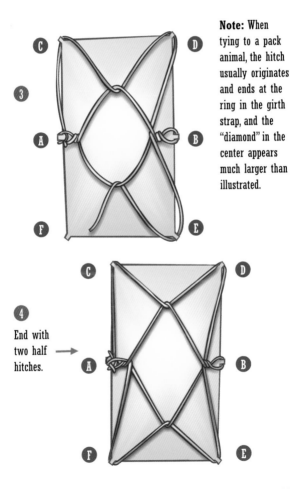

Figure 16. Figure Eight (End) Knot

Use this beautifully symmetric knot as a "stopper" knot on the end of a rope. It functions like an overhand knot, but with more bulk. The knot also makes a convenient slip noose for tying packages. When used in this manner, it is called the "packer's" or "parcel" knot.

Figure eight knot used as a slip knot for tying packages.

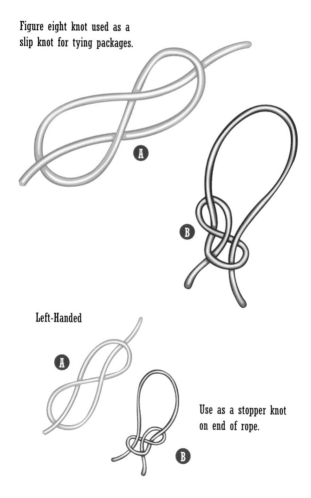

Left-Handed

Use as a stopper knot on end of rope.

Figure 17. Figure Eight Loop

The figure eight loop is a sort of schlocky bowline. It's easy to make, and it holds securely, even in slippery, synthetic rope (something that cannot be said of the bowline). If you need a quick, nonslip loop in the middle of a rope, the figure eight is much faster to make than a bowline on a bight. It's also ideal for putting a loop on hard-to-grasp twine and thread. However, the knot jams under load, so forget about untying it later. Use the figure eight loop for thin cordage; stick with the bowline for rope.

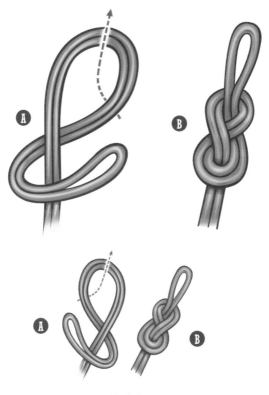

Left-Handed

Figure 18. Fisherman's Knot/
Double Fisherman's Knot

Once popular for tying leader to line, the fisherman's knot is now seldom used for this purpose because there are better knots for slippery nylon. Mountaineers like it for tying ropes together, however, because the knot has a finished, symmetrical look. Multiple coils (see S-knot, page 56) increase the security of the knot.

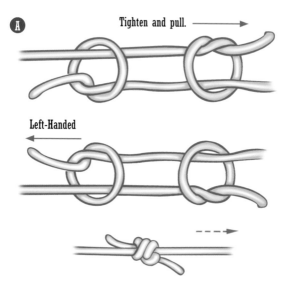

Tighten and pull.

Left-Handed

Canoeists and kayakers use the fisherman's knot to secure rope "grab loops" to the ends of their boats. Note: The knot is somewhat stronger when tied against the lay. If you wrap two turns around each rope, instead of just one, it is called the double fisherman's knot. (See S-knot, page 56).

Tighten and pull.

Figure 19A/B. One Half Hitch/ Two Half Hitches

Use two half hitches to tie a rope to a tree or a boat or animal to a ring. Sailors sometimes complete a clove hitch with one or two half hitches when they want infallible security. It's important that both half hitches are alike, as illustrated (i.e., both left- or right-handed). Half hitches are one of the most essential knots in macramé.

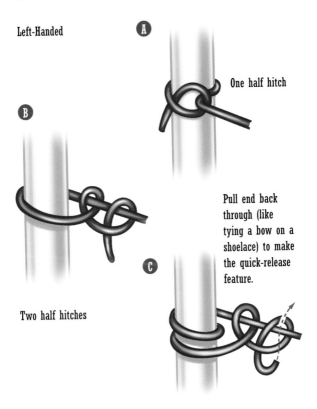

Left-Handed

A One half hitch

B

Two half hitches

Pull end back through (like tying a bow on a shoelace) to make the quick-release feature.

C

Two slippery half hitches and a round turn

Figure 19c. Two Slippery Half Hitches and a Round Turn

This is the quickest, most secure way to tie a boat or pack animal to a ring or bar. The "round turn" on the rail takes most of the stress off the basic knot. For faster removal, complete the hitch with a quick-release loop ("slippery" end), as illustrated.

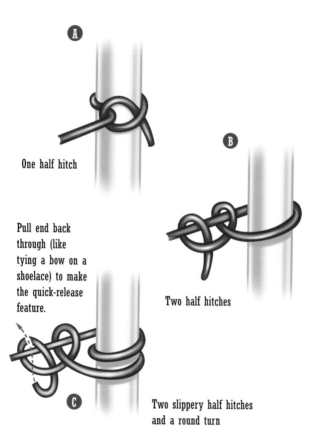

A

One half hitch

B

Pull end back through (like tying a bow on a shoelace) to make the quick-release feature.

Two half hitches

C

Two slippery half hitches and a round turn

Figure 20. Mooring Hitch

This knot looks like a slippery half hitch, but it's not. The mooring hitch holds fast under load yet comes apart instantly with a pull of the working end. You can tie it loosely and allow it to slide up to the rail like a slip knot, or jam the knot anywhere along its length so you can reach and release it without getting off your horse or out of your boat. This slick little hitch is well worth learning!

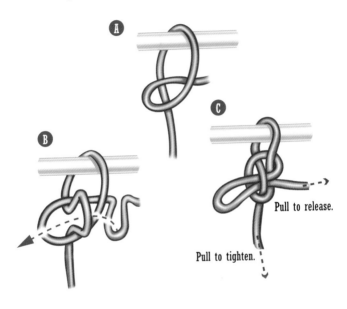

Pull to release.

Pull to tighten.

Left-Handed

Figure 21. Marline (Hammock) Hitch
(right-handed only)

Used by sailors for centuries to secure their hammock rolls, this easy hitch is handy for tying a long bedroll, package, or roll of carpeting. Be sure the marline end goes under each wrapping cord as illustrated. The hitch won't hold tension if you make it backward!

Right way

Wrong way

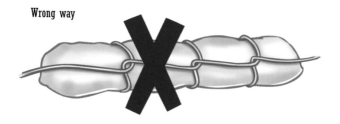

Figure 22. Monofilament Fishing Knot
(Clinch Knot)

Popular for tying lures to monofilament fishing line, this knot holds well and is easy to make, even with cold, stiff fingers. The breaking strength of the rope, with clinch knot applied, is about 80 percent the strength of the unknotted rope. Recommended by DuPont for use with nylon fishing line.

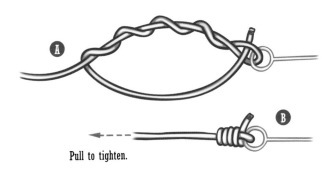

Pull to tighten.

Left-Handed

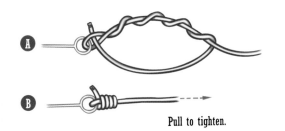

Pull to tighten.

Figure 23. Miller's (Constrictor) Knot

Similar to a clove hitch, the miller's knot is the fastest way to tie up a bulky sack. Be sure you run the first turn around the sack over the forefinger and the rest of the turns under it. When the coil is complete, grasp the working end B of the rope with your forefinger and pull it (tight) through the top loop as illustrated. For easy removal, complete the knot with a quick-release (slippery) loop.

Left-Handed

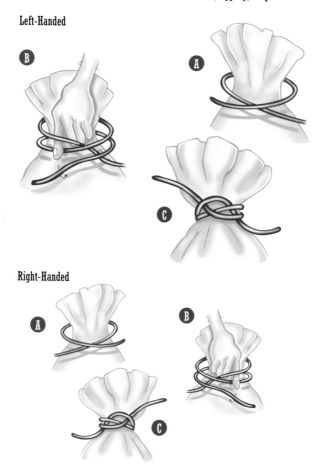

Right-Handed

Figure 24. Pipe Hitch

This simple hitch is great for lifting a pipe or post vertically out of the ground. It won't slip, even on metal pipe. Simply take four or five turns around the post, cross the wrappings, and end with a pair of half hitches. Finish off with another half hitch high on the post (same way you complete a timber hitch) to keep the post vertical when pulling.

One half hitch

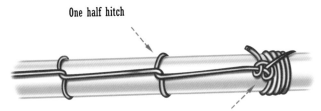

Two half hitches

Figure 25. Prussik Knot (right-handed only)

Use the prussik knot whenever you want an absolutely secure loop that won't slip along a tight line. Mountaineers use this knot for footholds to help them climb a vertical rope. The prussik loop slides easily along a tight rope, yet it jams solidly when a load (horizontal or vertical) is applied. I've found this knot useful for rigging rainflies in camp and for rescuing rock-pinned canoes in a river. Make the loop from a length of parachute cord, completed with a fisherman's knot.

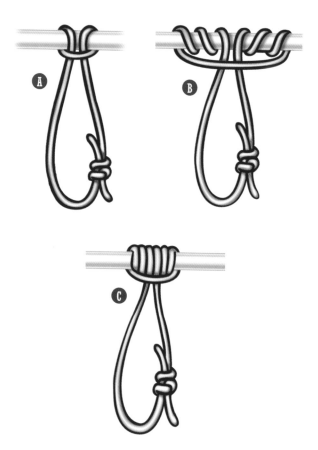

Figure 26. Sheepshank

Problem: Your rope has a length of worn section in the middle. Eventually, you'll get around to splicing it, but for now, it will have to be used as is. The solution is the sheepshank—an ancient knot used by sailors to shorten rope that's too long for the job at hand.

The sheepshank holds only when there is tension at each end; even then, it sometimes fails. For this reason, it is best to secure it by inserting sticks of wood through the end loops as illustrated.

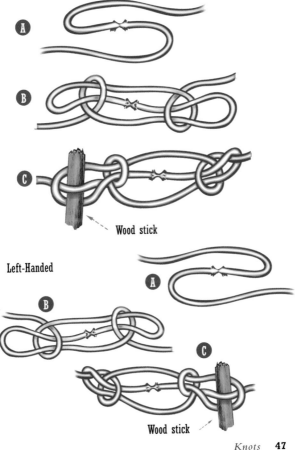

A

B

C

Wood stick

Left-Handed

A

B

C

Wood stick

Figure 27. Power Cinch (Trucker's Knot)

The power cinch is the most ingenious hitch to come along in recent years. It effectively replaces the taut-line hitch and functions as a powerful pulley. Skilled canoeists use this pulley knot almost exclusively for tying canoes on cars, and it remains popular with truckers for securing heavy loads. Use it anytime you need to tie an object tightly onto a car top or truck bed.

Begin the hitch by forming the overhand loop shown above in step 1. Pull the loop through, as in step 2. It is important that you make the loop exactly as shown. It will look okay if you make it backward, but it won't work!

If you're tying something onto a car top, run the working end of the hitch through an S-hook attached to the bumper (steps 3 and 4).

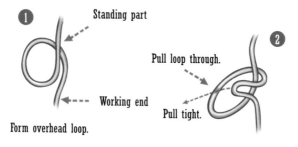

1 Standing part

Working end

Form overhead loop.

2 Pull loop through.

Pull tight.

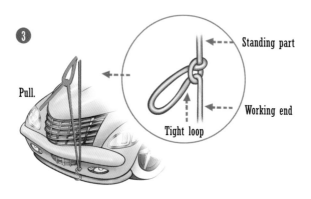

3 Pull.

Standing part

Working end

Tight loop

Snug the hitch and secure it with a pair of half hitches around the bight, as illustrated in step 6a. Or, for ease of removal, end the power cinch with a quick-release half hitch, as in steps 5 and 6.

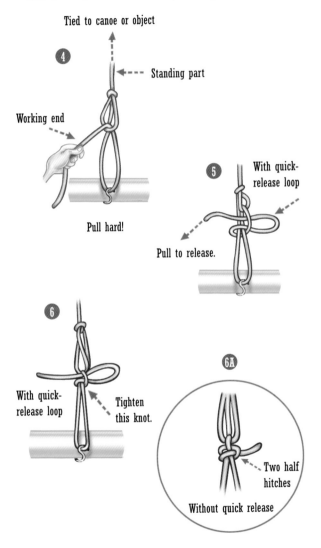

Tied to canoe or object

4

Standing part

Working end

Pull hard!

5

With quick-release loop

Pull to release.

6

With quick-release loop

Tighten this knot.

6A

Two half hitches

Without quick release

The power cinch as a multiple pulley: For additional power, as in the above scenario, form a second loop in the working end of the rope, as shown in step 7. This will double the mechanical advantage, although it will increase friction. This rescue technique—commonly set up with aluminum carabiners instead of rope loops—was popularized by the Nantahala Outdoor Center (a whitewater canoe and kayak school) as the "Z-drag," because the rope pattern forms a lazy Z when viewed from overhead.

The basic power cinch, however, is probably all you'll ever need. I consider it the most useful hitch there is.

7 SUPER-SECURE VERSION

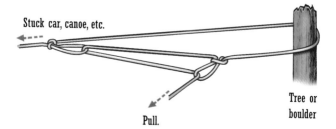

Stuck car, canoe, etc.

Tree or boulder

Pull.

AS A MULTIPLE PULLEY

Figure 28. Quick-Release (Slippery) Loop

Nothing is more frustrating than untying a bunch of tight knots when you're breaking camp in the morning. If you end your knots with a "quick-release" (slippery) loop, as illustrated, you'll be able to untie your ties with a single pull. Form the quick-release feature by running the working end of the rope back through the completed knot—the same as making a "bow" when you tie your shoes.

Use a simple overhand knot with a slippery loop to seal drawstring bags and stuff sacks. The plastic "cord-locks" sold in stores for this purpose are for people who don't know how to tie slippery knots.

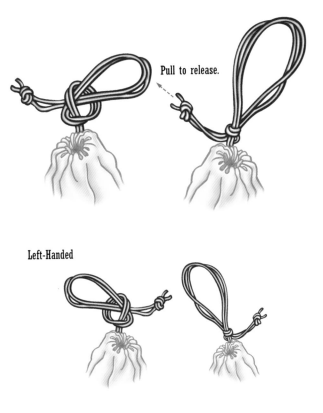

Pull to release.

Left-Handed

Figure 29. Sheet Bend/Double Sheet Bend/ Slippery Sheet Bend

The sheet bend is one of the most useful knots and one of the few that can be used for tying two ropes together, even when rope sizes and materials differ greatly. It's important that the working ends of the sheet bend be on the same side, as illustrated; otherwise the knot will be unreliable. If you want the knot to release instantly, end it with a quick-release (slippery) half hitch (figure 29b). For greater security, especially in plastic rope, use the double sheet bend (Becket bend). It's the same as the single version but with an extra coil around the standing loop (figure 29c).

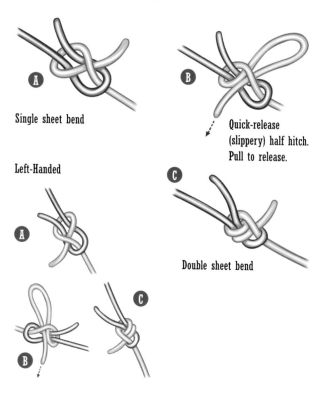

Single sheet bend

Quick-release (slippery) half hitch. Pull to release.

Left-Handed

Double sheet bend

Figure 30. Sliding Figures of Eight

This easy bend will join two ropes of unequal thickness. The ropes won't slip when a load is applied. Sliding figures of eight performs the same task as the classic sheet bend (see page 52), but it's easier to untie when the rope has been subjected to a heavy load. Make the figure eights as illustrated, then pull them tight and slide them together. The bond strengthens as tension is applied. To undo the knot, grab the short working ends of the figure eights and pull them apart. The knots will untie easily when they are separated.

Figure 31. Spanish Bowline

This neat knot is similar to a bowline on a bight. The series of loops make a rather uncomfortable chair or backyard swing. Center the rope and form the three loops illustrated in step 1. Then, fold the large middle loop down (step 2). Next, enlarge the loop so the two smaller loops are inside (step 3). Now pull the ears of the large loops through the ears in the smaller loops, as shown in step 4. Pull the knot to tighten, and your chair is complete.

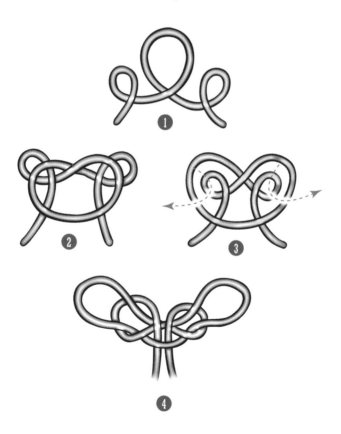

Figure 32. Strap Knot

The strap knot isn't a knot per se but a handy method of tying leather or nylon straps together to form a long rope. It's nothing more than a single half hitch, each made opposite to the other.

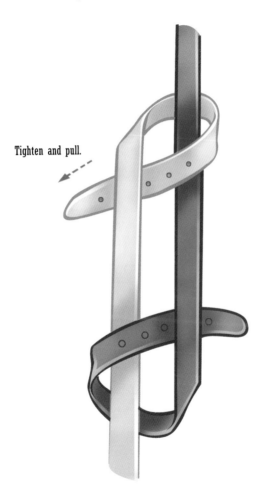

Tighten and pull.

Figure 33. S-Knot

Here's an artistic way to tie two ropes together. Similar to a fisherman's knot, the S-knot has more coils and so is probably more secure, especially in slippery ropes.

Place the ends of the rope parallel to one another and take three or more complete turns around the two ropes, then run the working (free) end down the center of the knot. Do the same with the other rope. Finally, slide the knots together to complete the S-knot.

Note: If you wrap two turns around each rope, it is called the double fisherman's knot.

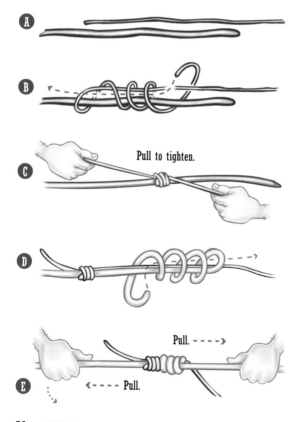

A

B

C Pull to tighten.

D

E Pull. - - - - >

< - - - - Pull.

Figure 34. Square (Reef) Knot

For centuries sailors have used the square knot for reefing sails and tying things aboard ship. It is still used for this purpose but probably more popular for tying packages, gauze dressings, tourniquets, and other medical applications. Don't use this knot for joining two ropes together if they will be under load! The square knot jams under tension and falls apart (it becomes two half hitches) if the ropes are very dissimilar or the pull comes unevenly. Use a sheet bend, fisherman's knot, or two bowlines for joining ropes. To form a square knot rather than a common granny knot, complete each overhand knot opposite the other. Thus, if the first knot is formed right-handed (right over left), the second must be made left-handed (left over right).

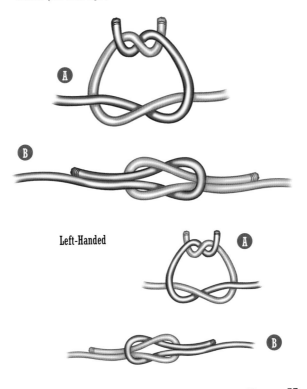

Left-Handed

Figure 35. Surgeon's Knot

Simply a square knot with an extra turn on the bottom and perhaps an additional turn on top (there are two forms of the knot as illustrated). The surgeon's knot is much more secure in slippery materials than the traditional square knot. Whitewater kayakers use a slippery surgeon's knot (with quick-release loop) to tie the slick nylon waist ties of their life jackets.

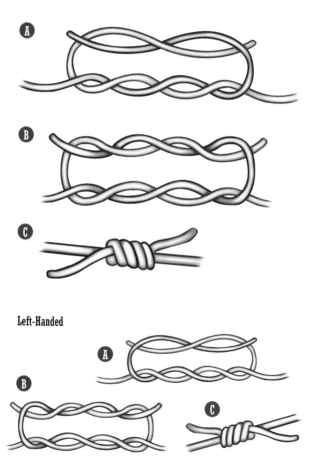

Left-Handed

Figure 36. Taut-Line (Rolling) Hitch

Sailors use the rolling hitch whenever they want to attach a rope to a spar. The knot is much more secure than a clove hitch, especially when the load is parallel to the spar.

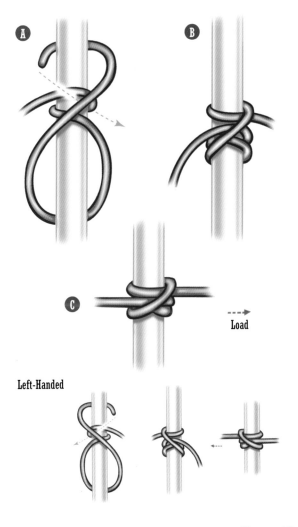

Load

Left-Handed

The hitch can be applied to a tight rope that's secured around a tree or tent stake, in which case it is called the "taut-line hitch." Boy Scouts prefer the taut-line hitch for anchoring their tent guylines. The hitch slides freely yet jams under load.

The original (rolling) hitch is a fine knot for its intended purpose. However, it is less versatile and much inferior to the more powerful power cinch (trucker's knot) explained on page 48.

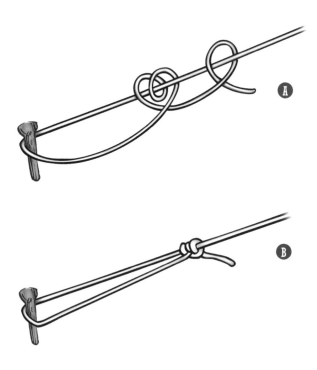

Figure 37. Timber Hitch (right-handed only)

Use the timber hitch for hauling logs, timbers, heavy pipe, and cumbersome objects. It's very strong (about 70 percent), won't slip, and it can't jam, no matter how heavy the load. I often attach the towrope to my Jeep with a timber hitch when clearing brush and trees. It always comes apart easily. It's best to complete the timber hitch with a half hitch near the hauling end to keep a long log from twisting.

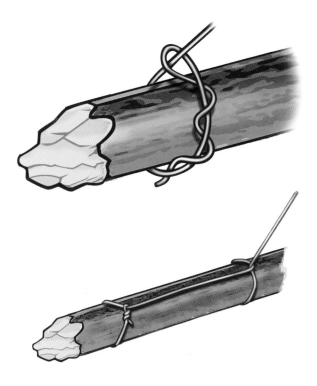

Figure 38. Trilene (Fishing) Knot

Berkeley researchers recommend this knot for tying lures in slippery monofilament line. The trilene knot is a cross between an anchor bend and a clinch knot. Berkeley tests reveal that the knot yields 80 to 90 percent of the line's breaking strength. **Tip:** Wet the knot before tightening it; this will lubricate the line and reduce damage caused by the heat of friction.

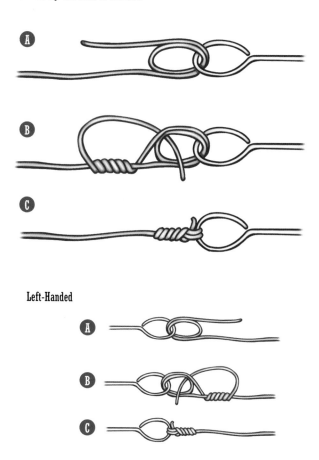

Left-Handed

Splices

Figure 39. Eye Splice

You can form a loop at the end of a line with a bowline, but it's not nearly as strong as an eye splice. And when it comes to beauty, there's no contest between a bulky knot and a symmetrical splice.

(1) Whip the rope (optional) about 6 inches from the end and unravel the strands labeled **A** **B** **C**. (2) Form a loop (eye) and begin the splice, weaving the strands through **A** **B** **C** as illustrated.

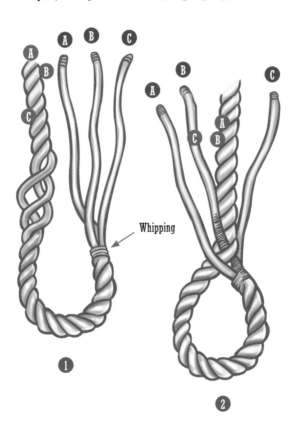

Whipping

Note that each strand is tucked through the rope from right to left, against the lay. Twist the strands clockwise as you pull them through the rope and maintain the same tension on each strand. This will give the splice a smooth, untwisted look. Splicing will go easier if you have a pointed tool to open the lay.

(4) Reverse the splice and tuck **C** under **C**.

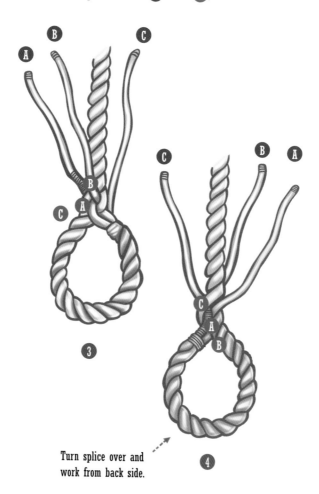

Turn splice over and
work from back side.

(5) Reverse splice again and continue to weave the strands as shown. You may continue to splice until the strands are all buried (maximum strength is reached with three tucks), or snip off each strand a tuck or two apart to taper the finished splice (more artistic).

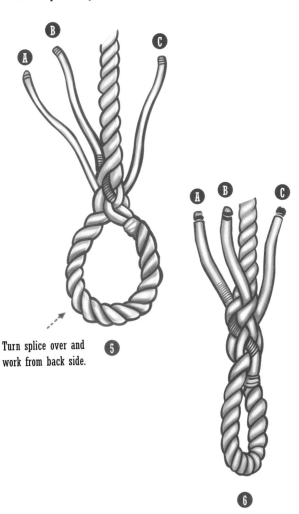

Turn splice over and work from back side.

Finish by rolling the splice firmly between your hands. Flame-whip the ends of the protruding strands (synthetic line) and roll again. Cut off the temporary whipping, and your splice is complete.

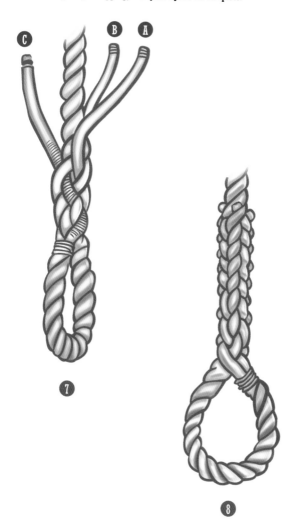

Figure 40. Short Splice

This is the strongest way to join two ropes. It reduces the line's breaking strength by about 10 percent.

(1) Untwist the strands of each rope a half dozen turns, then, "marry" alternating strands together.

(2) To keep the "nonworking" strands temporarily out of the way, you may want to lightly whip or tape them to the rope body. Some sailors also tape the ends of each strand to keep them from unraveling.

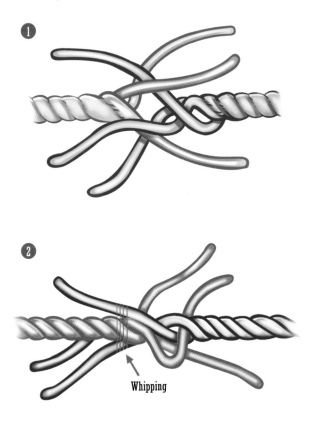

Whipping

The rest of the splice is academic: Simply tuck each strand alternately against the lay of the rope, as illustrated. Three or four tucks ensure maximum strength, but you can make the splice as long as you like.

Finish by rolling the completed splice briskly between your hands, then flame-whip (synthetic rope) the exposed strand ends. A final roll between your hands or underfoot rounds up the splice.

3

4

Lashings

Figure 41. Square Lashing

Use this classic lashing to secure two spars that touch each other at the point where they cross. Begin the lashing with a clove hitch or timber hitch around the vertical spar, just below the cross piece **A**. Run the cord over the horizontal bar **B**, around behind the vertical bar, then back over the face of the horizontal bar on the left. Tighten snugly, then bring the cord behind the vertical bar and up the right

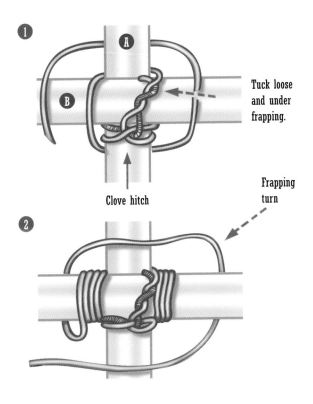

Tuck loose and under frapping.

Clove hitch

Frapping turn

front side of the horizontal bar. Repeat this three or four times. Finish with two "frapping" (binding) turns to tighten the lashing and lock everything in place with a clove hitch on the crosspiece.

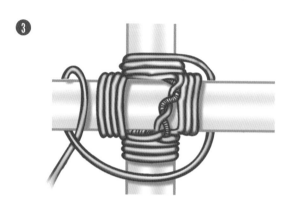

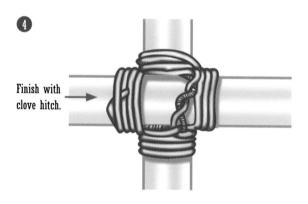

Finish with clove hitch.

Figure 42. Tripod Lashing

Here's a fast, secure way to make a support for a camera or coffeepot. If you end the lashing with a quick-release (slippery) clove hitch, it will come undone instantly.

Lay out the spars on the ground with the center spar pointing away from the other two. Begin with a clove hitch or timber hitch at the end of one of the side spars. Then, make six to eight loose turns around all three spars and finish up with two frapping (binding) turns between each spar. A clove hitch on the center bar completes the lashing.

Note: The sheer lashing (not illustrated)—which is used to secure parallel spars in bridges and tables—is simply a two-legged version of the tripod lashing.

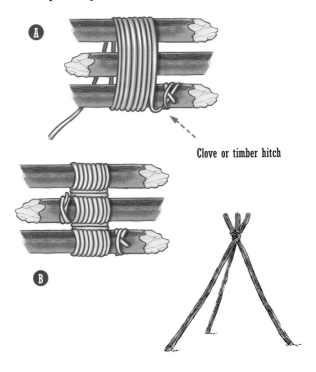

Clove or timber hitch

About the Author

Cliff Jacobson is one of North America's most respected outdoors writers and wilderness canoe guides. He is a retired environmental science teacher, an outdoors skills instructor, a canoeing and camping consultant, and the author of more than a dozen top-selling books on canoeing and camping. He is a recipient of the American Canoe Association's prestigious Legends of Paddling Award and a member of the ACA Hall of Fame. He lives in River Falls, Wisconsin.